Volume 105 of the Yale Series of Younger Poets

for my mother and father

CONTENTS

The human fascination with beauty has produced many acts of tribute and imitation but relatively few insights, possibly because what transpires in the presence of beauty occurs in a mind initially mesmerized or stunned. Other sensations follow, none of them articulate: first a rush of excitement, this succeeded by a feeling of arrival, of completeness, and with this new completeness, insatiability—the enslaved attention refuses to relinquish its object. The hand (for example) cannot turn the page.

This power to stun the mind has diminished the prestige of beauty in literary discourse. It compels awe, and awe is well known for its capacity to silence. Here is nothing of the sort of puzzle or dilemma the mind prefers. Quite the opposite: beauty seems a sort of all-purpose solution to everything, obviating the debate and argument by which the mind is energized. In consequence, it disappears from debate: by both poets and critics, it is mentioned offhandedly or apologetically, as an incidental virtue or mild defect, unlikely to advance philosophical understanding. It exists—serene, impervious—beyond or apart from the vicissitudes of fashion; it cannot be achieved in the laboratories of ingenuity or craft. Miraculous, and also patently at odds with the play of intellect which (no matter how labored or how trivial) monopolizes contemporary attention and stimulates elaborate response. Numinous and clear, the beautiful offends the mind with its quality of self-sufficiency or finality.

Nowhere is this schism between public approbation and secret power more intensely played out than in lyric poetry. This is one of

Keats's great themes: to suggest that beauty subverts the mind is not to suggest that its appeal is fundamentally or exclusively to the senses. It speaks to some abiding longing: for the pure, for the apparently whole. Song directed "not to the sensual ear"—in its presence, the suspicious reader is both helpless and exalted (not, I would say, cerebral responses). In such moments, the poem seems not a relic but an absolute. Time, narrative time, is abolished. The only close parallel is falling in love:

The late cranes throwing
their necks to the wind stay
somewhere between
the place that rain begins
and the place that it ends
they seem to exist just there
above the horizon at least
I only see them that way
tossed up
against the gray October
light not heavy enough
for feet to be useful or
useless enough to make
gravity untie its string. I'm sick
of this stubbornness
but the earthworms
seem to think it all right
they move forward
and let the world pass
through them they eat
and eat at it, content to connect
everything through
the individual links
of their purple bodies to stay
one place would be death.
But somewhere between
the crane and the worm

between the days I pass through
and the days that pass
through me
in the mind. And memory
which outruns the body and
grief which arrests it.   —"Statuary"

How vulnerable it seems, this poem, how fragile: a narrow col-
umn of awareness, its movement too perpetual or too transfixed to
seem headlong, despite its unpunctuated urgencies. The elemental
grandeur of the oppositions—birth and death, heaven and earth,
crane and worm—and of the mimetic structure, the explicit lesson
that "to stay / one place would be death": these could veer close to
parody or sentimentality were it not for Katherine Larson's grace
and simplicity, her eerie purity of tone. "Statuary" (like most of the
poems in *Radial Symmetry*) moves toward synthesis and repose (ra-
ther than toward ecstatic disintegration), toward containment as
opposed to release. But containment and repose do not imply, here,
a placid summary or moral. Larson's repose is also a quivering
suspension, in which multiple perceptions, multiple elements, are
held in extended and mysterious relation. The shape is classic; in
"Statuary" Larson has not so much made something new as she has
given form to ancient knowledge.

This is a poem of great beauty. But beauty is also Larson's sub-
ject. So much of earth is here, at once utterly natural and wholly
illumined: a grave passivity infuses this collection; experience is
less sought than received. The poet is a kind of dazed Miranda, so
new to the world that its every ordinariness seems an emblem of
wonder. "Either everything's sublime or nothing is," she writes,
and for the span of the book, everything is.

Larson trained as a biologist, but these poems do not seem (at
least to a layman) a scientist's work. They prize sensation over
analytic scrutiny, the individual example over the category. Her
education in science manifests here as a passion for detail (as well as
a richness of reference): "I know I'm still alive because I love / to
eat," she says, and everywhere in this work is the sensualist's grate-

ful and specific avidity. The longest poem in the book, "Ghost Nets," makes a kind of dreamlike diary of being; the precision and variety of Larson's impressions, their layered abundance, correspond to the gleanings of some very lucky (and actual) nets. The implications of the title also make of the poem a protest: an informed defense of unprotected life in the face of casually pervasive human destructiveness. Each section seems a gift, an instance of harmoniousness between consciousness and flesh, the scientist's fastidious attention to detail suffused with an unexpected gentleness or solicitude toward matter:

> *Yellow snapper, bright as egg yolk.* I look at the sea and eat my toast.
>
> Yesterday's lesson—the *jabonero de Cortés* or Cortez soapfish
> when agitated
> secretes a mucus that lathers like soap—
>
> —"Ghost Nets / I"

and this:

> "Not perfection," the sea hisses, "but originality." The innards
> of a blue-eyed scallop scraped onto a plastic Safeway bag.
> Soul and meat—
>
> —"Ghost Nets / V"

and this:

> Every day, it happens like this.
> We emerge from the pale nets of sleep like ghost shrimp
> in the estuaries—
> The brain humming its electric language.
>
> Touching something in a state of becoming.
>
> —"Ghost Nets / VII"

and this:

> I remember Agassiz and the sunfish. The dream in which each
> breath is a perfect sphere, in which the only explanation is
> pink and voltaic—

life! Sealed inside itself like barnacles at high tide.

. . . .

Down the road, large piles of murex shells—
        their insides like the insides of ears.

                   —"Ghost Nets / VIII"

Sequence and consequence, the drama of unfolding story, play almost no role here. Nor is data organized into argument. Rather events and images are held together in some fluid medium which preserves them without changing them: the whole sequence has the fascination of a prism. Or perhaps the spectacle of a cell under a microscope with its unfolding revelations.

Intense sensation—I suppose the accurate word is pleasure—is not subjected to overt judgment or intervention. But the book as a whole is far less celebratory, less contented, than this description suggests. Larson's passion for detail carries with it, for poet as well as reader, awareness of the transience of matter, so these luminous poems give off an atmosphere of forboding: darkness is omnipresent, encroaching.

This is especially pronounced in the love poems; erotic ravenousness is mirrored in the rapacious greed of the spirits: " . . . everywhere the spirits are hungry," she writes:

Say you leave a crust of bread on your plate.
A hundred of them could last for weeks on this.

If you said a prayer with your meal,
the offering might feed a multitude.
But then the sea always asks for more.

The speaker remembers the evening, dinner with her lover:

Sawdust floors. A mussel split and rusty
against the polished ebony of the bowl,

its sea smell like the beach at low tide . . .

And later:

She is suddenly aware of her desire for him

across the table, next to him on the bus.
But it makes her shiver, the way
those shells split apart—like half-black

moons that gave off no light, only
shadows. And they were legion.

—"Low Tide Evening"

Excerpts cannot give a sense of the power such lines have in a
poem that has taken its time accruing. Pacing is essential: the
gravity of these unequivocal, summarizing assertions depends ab-
solutely on the sustained images and vignettes that precede them.
Statement, as it works here, has the force of inescapable truth. The
last section of the four-part "Love at Thirty-two Degrees" is an
example, particularly stunning in its succinctness. Here, in part, is
the section preceding:

Then, there is the astronomer's wife
ascending stairs to her bed.

The astronomer gazes out,
one eye at a time,

to a sky that expands
even as it falls apart

like a paper boat dissolving in bilge.

. . . .

The snow outside

is white and quiet
as a woman's slip

against cracked floorboards.
So he walks to the house

inflamed by moonlight, and slips
into the bed with his wife

her hair and arms all
in disarray

like fish confused by waves.

The final section follows:

Science—

beyond pheromones, hormones, aesthetics of bone,
every time I make love for love's sake alone,

I betray you.

This is a collection notable for its variety: formal, tonal, and—
strikingly—environmental. It occurred to me that most poets who
are, like Katherine Larson, deeply attuned to the natural world tend
to be specifically attuned to a particular landscape. *Radial Symmetry*
has no one context; its shifting backgrounds take the place of mo-
tion giving the collection a feeling of progression or drama, as
though movement in space substituted for movement in time. The
effect suggests the old Hollywood mechanics of action: the driver
and the passenger in the stationary car while the background
lurches wildly forward and the wind machine blows apace. In a
collection of poems remarkable for the stillness of the individual
lyrics, such variety of setting suggests the conveyor belt, a relentless
momentum alluding to the brevity or insufficiency of human life.

The overall dreamlike ambiance of this work is vividly inter-
rupted, here and there, by poems rooted in literal (or brilliantly
invented) dreams—on display in such poems is a pointed and se-
ductive wit:

In the dream, I am given a monkey heart
and told to be careful how I love
because of the resulting infection.

and later:

A voice says, *Metamorphosis
will make you ugly. . . .*

We find ourselves, soon enough, "On the lawn of my childhood house, / an operating table, doctors, / a patient under a sheet. . . ." When the sheet is lifted:

> It isn't my mother. It's the monkey.
> I bend my ear to its dying lips
> and it says: *You haven't much time—*
> *risk it all.*

Wise monkey. There are other dreams, one, notably, involving Baudelaire and Margaret Mead.

But ultimately, I think, a reader will remember these poems for their beauty, the profound sense of being in the present that their sensuality embodies, and a sense, too, of its cost.

Poetry survives because it haunts and it haunts because it is simultaneously utterly clear and deeply mysterious; because it cannot be entirely accounted for, it cannot be exhausted. The poems in *Radial Symmetry* are comparatively direct, accessible, easy to read. But Katherine Larson has that gift Yeats had, what Keats had, a power to enthrall the ear, and the ear is stubborn, easily as stubborn as the mind: it will not let this voice go:

> The Milky Way sways its back
> across all of wind-eaten America
> like a dusty saddle tossed
> over your sable, lunatic horse.
> All the plains are dark.
> All the stars are cowards:
> they lie to us about their time of death
> and do nothing but dangle
> like a huge chandelier
> over nights when our mangled sobs
> make the dead reach for their guns.
> I must be one of the only girls
> who still dreams in green gingham, sees snow
> as *a steel pail's falling of frozen nails*
> like you said through pipe smoke

on the cabin porch one night. Dear one,
there are no nails more cold
than those that fix you
underground. I thought I saw you
in the moon of the auditorium
after my high school dance.
Without you, it's still hard to dance.
It's even hard to dream.

—"Broke the Lunatic Horse"

Louise Glück

ACKNOWLEDGMENTS

Grateful acknowledgment is made to the editors of the publications in which the following poems, sometimes in slightly different forms, first appeared:

AGNI: "Masculine/Feminine," "Study for Love's Body"; *Alaska Quarterly Review*: "In a Cemetery by the Sea: One Definition of a Circle"; *Boulevard*: "Broke the Lunatic Horse"; *Ekphrasis*: "Preparing for Sleep"; *El Nacional* (Venezuela): "The Gardens in Tunisia"; *The Kenyon Review*: "Crypsis and Mimicry," "Lake of Little Birds"; *KROnline:* "Metamorphosis," "Solarium"; *The Massachusetts Review*: "Risk"; *Notre Dame Review*: versions of "Ghost Nets" published as "Three Ghost Nets"; *Poetry*: "Almost a Figure," "Love at Thirty-two Degrees," "Low Tide Evening," "Patience," "Statuary."

"Love at Thirty-two Degrees" was featured by *Poetry Daily*. "Statuary" was republished in *Literature: An Introduction to Reading and Writing* (9th Edition), ed. Edgar V. Roberts (Upper Saddle River, NJ: Prentice Hall, 2008).

Special thanks to Louise Glück for supporting this work: her insight and generosity have been truly inspiring. Thanks to my teachers, Rita Dove, Gregory Orr, Boyer Rickel, and Charles Wright, and to Natalie Bryant Rizzieri, Danielle Chapman, and Jamison Crabtree for their close readings of these poems. Further gratitude to The Poetry Foundation, whose Ruth Lilly Poetry Fellowship allowed me to live and work at the Sea of Cortez, and to Heather Green: both made "Ghost Nets" possible. Finally, I'm deeply indebted to my extraordinary family, and to Alex, who notices butterflies.

ONE

STATUARY

The late cranes throwing
their necks to the wind stay
somewhere between
the place that rain begins
and the place that it ends
they seem to exist just there
above the horizon at least
I only see them that way
tossed up
against the gray October
light not heavy enough
for feet to be useful or
useless enough to make
gravity untie its string. I'm sick
of this stubbornness
but the earthworms
seem to think it all right
they move forward
and let the world pass
through them they eat
and eat at it, content to connect
everything through
the individual links
of their purple bodies to stay
one place would be death.
But somewhere between
the crane and the worm
between the days I pass through

and the days that pass
through me
is the mind. And memory
which outruns the body and
grief which arrests it.

LOW TIDE EVENING

On the bus from the west coast of Ireland,
a woman stares past rain pooling on the window.
Clover fields hemmed in by rough stone.

The man next to her has fingers trapped
in a botanical book; he sleeps. She knows
that south of Galway, where they strayed

through terraced shales and grey-blue
limestones searching for fossils, the sea
licks pale lichens off the rocks

and everywhere the spirits are hungry.
Say you leave a crust of bread on your plate.
A hundred of them could last for weeks on this.

If you said a prayer with your meal,
the offering might feed a multitude.
But then the sea always asks for more.

She closes her eyes. The cool consequence
of creatures that glided through ancient seabeds.
I travel half the world and still I feel chased.

She thinks of dinner with the man.
Sawdust floors. A mussel split and rusty
against the polished ebony of the bowl,

its sea smell like the beach at low tide,
walking through the inhuman hour
when the world resolves into a single blue pane

of stained glass, the gulls and shadows
involved with one thing only: hunger.
She is suddenly aware of her desire for him

across the table, next to him on the bus.
But it makes her shiver, the way
those shells split apart—like half-black

moons that gave off no light, only
shadows. And they were legion.

STUDY FOR LOVE'S BODY

I. *Landscape with Yellow Birds*

The theories of Love
have become tremulous and complicated.
The way snow falls or Saturn revolves
repeatedly around some distance
where space is nothing
yet still something that separates.

Never mind time. Caterpillars
have turned the fruit trees
into body bags. The children paint
the mandibles of fallen ones with
silver meant for nursery stars.
Without the immense responsibility
of sympathy, these small deaths
are nothing more than
artifice. Like a single magnolia
in a cut glass bowl
we have no idea where
our roots went so suddenly.

II. *Architecture in Ruins*

Third floor of the doll factory,
ferns suck carbon
and sharper chemicals from air
near the women working.

They're hunched over tables
of warped wood.
Half of everyone is painting
eyes and lashes on porcelain heads, the rest
are threading hands to sleeves.

Outside in the courtyard
a smattering of doves rise.
Have you ever wanted to
kiss a stranger's hands?

III. *Gardens Without Bats or Moss*

Gauguin writes to Theo van Gogh that in his painting he wants to suggest
the idea of suffering—without ever explaining what kind.

IV. *In Stone Archways*

The light is spilt green milk, which is languorous
as the red monkey Gauguin painted

by the brown body of Anna
the Javanese. At the Chinese Market

I buy two red teacups and a can
of coconut milk. I think—

Gauguin wouldn't know
how Anna loved that monkey

and sang to him late at night.
Everywhere the sea screams

at me. A great pink slab of octopus arm,
beside it, babies seasoned in orange spices.

Such symmetry! Surely they swam
through the night like thirsty

flowers. I think you had it right
when you said love is the mathematics

of distance. Split like a clam on ice,
I feel raw, half-eaten. I rot

in the cold blue of the ego,
the crushed velvet of Anna's chair.

PREPARING FOR SLEEP

—after Rousseau

Water snakes fall from her mouth like a knot of silk
loosed. Fire is no companion here, the voice says
to her, the small moon a pot of boiling milk

that keeps pouring into her dress. At night before bed
he fills a glass of water, unbuttons his shabby coat.
Against the plaster in the corner, the portrait

of Apollinaire salutes. *Le Douanier* wanders alone
through *Le Jardin des Plantes,* Paris. Listening for the hoof
of water in the thick, dark stems, the form

by which thirst hauls itself from the ground. On the roof
of his flat, he paints in the herbarium. Lying
on the pink divan where he can't stare enough

at the jungle that arranges its foliage against the day
so naturally. It plays for him, is never quite the same:
bromeliads uncurl, strange beasts pad in with moonlit eyes,

a spoonbill tiptoes past and is arrested into frame.
The paintbrush renders. Poverty fatigues. But between
parallel lives he finds he's deeply happy, unashamed

of his eccentricities and need to paint things
to which no one attaches belief.
The dark woman returns each night to his dreams

with a mandolin, stretched against dunes and fast asleep.
Someday, he thinks, my chest could be opened
by a switchblade. I'd die in the gutter of this street.

But in the drain where my heart might have been
they'll find Chopin on the phonograph, a woman
magnetized by sleep and hunted by lions in terrible skins.

CRYPSIS AND MIMICRY

Crypsis for the way that things are hidden.
How certain small truths disappear against
a larger truth. The way my Cajun friend explains
bouillabaisse as the synthesis of red snapper and crab,
oysters, mussels, and crayfish. Garlic and orange
peel. Dry white wine. A *fusion of the senses.*
So autumn slips into the swamplands
with glossy alligator eyes. We talk of love potions
while drinking *café noir.* Powdered lizards
and tender missives scrawled with blood. How her
grandmother crushed peach seeds with stones
to draw dirt to the bottom of a pail of bayou water:
a speckled fish could flatten itself against those
sediments and simply fade away. She used to dream
there was a hole in the bucket and so the task
was never-ending. That's crypsis—
everything against intrinsic terrain dissolves in it.
Mimicry is different. It's you stroking my throat
as if I'm a bird. It's me pretending in your arms to *be* a bird.
I am not a bird. I remember reading how the Curies' laboratory
would glow at night; Marie wrote
of the enchantment of those luminous silhouettes.
I used to believe that science was only concerned
with certainty. Later, I recognized its mystery.
There isn't language for it—
The way I can see you when you are shining.
Our roots crypsis, our wings mimicry.

A LIME TREE FOR SAN CRISTÓBAL

—the Galápagos

On this island, all the tortoises are priests
of an exclusive past. What other living thing
survives on prickly pear and guava? The pure
sting of citrus delivers perfume in a halo
of blossoms.

      My carpentry here is rough
and leaves me dreaming of Spanish arches.
If there's anything a coast imparts, it's patience
with imperfect lines.

          Today's specimen: *Eel dark
reddish purplish brown with pale or whitish
brown spots.*

      I know I'm still alive because I love
to eat. On the table's a gift
from fishermen: pink gills embroidered
blood, the eyes—two mirrors snapped over
with iron. This shark that I will cut and soak
in lime has a mouth made for eating darkness—
an architecture built without a need for dawn.

LOVE AT THIRTY-TWO DEGREES

I

Today I dissected a squid,
the late acacia tossing its pollen
across the black of the lab bench.
In a few months the maples
will be bleeding. That was the thing:
there was no blood
only textures of gills folded like satin,
suction cups like planets in rows. *Be careful
not to cut your finger,* he says. But I'm thinking
of fingertips on my lover's neck
last June. Amazing, hearts.
This branchial heart. After class,
I stole one from the formaldehyde
and watched it bloom in my bathroom sink
between the cubes of ice.

II

Last night I threw my lab coat in the fire
and drove all night through the Arizona desert
with a thermos full of silver tequila.

It was the last of what we bought
on our way back from Guadalajara—
desert wind in the mouth, your mother's
beat-up Honda, agaves
twisting up from the soil
like the limbs of cephalopods.

Outside of Tucson, saguaros so lovely
considering the cold, and the fact that you
weren't there to warm me.
Suddenly drunk I was shouting that I wanted to see the stars
as my ancestors used to see them—

To see the godawful blue as Aurvandil's frostbitten toe.

III

Then, there is the astronomer's wife
ascending stairs to her bed.

The astronomer gazes out,
one eye at a time,

to a sky that expands
even as it falls apart

like a paper boat dissolving in bilge.
Furious, fuming stars.

When his migraine builds and
lodges its dark anchor behind

the eyes, he fastens the wooden buttons
of his jacket, and walks

outside with a flashlight
to keep company with the barn owl

who stares back at him with eyes
that are no greater or less than

a spiral galaxy.
The snow outside

is white and quiet
as a woman's slip

against cracked floorboards.
So he walks to the house

inflamed by moonlight, and slips
into the bed with his wife

her hair and arms all
in disarray

like fish confused by waves.

IV

Science—

beyond pheromones, hormones, aesthetics of bone,
every time I make love for love's sake alone,

I betray you.

TWO

THE GARDENS IN TUNISIA

A single day is enough to make us a little larger or,
another time, a little smaller.
>   —Paul Klee

There is a long wave of pleasure
in the sideways red house.
And a sun so round it might exhale.
Cranes that cut the hands of water
with their sudden flight.

You'll find a thread unfurling
to the arrogant volcano, who is decorated
with defunct medals and wants
to explain to you the color white,
its terrible infidelity.

Yes, Paul, I spend too much money.
I cheat on everyone I love.
My tired letters shuffle through dusk
like summer insects.

There are days that walk through me
and I cannot hold them.

So I fall in love with the man in the moon.
He makes the tide uncover me. Then takes off
his glasses and explains, "I've brought you
this gift: the starkness of my hands and
the crater of my mouth."

LAKE OF LITTLE BIRDS

Let me begin with the lepers at Lake Bunyonyi.

They were cured, but blind
and terribly disfigured. Their island overgrown
with scarlet poinsettias.

A school, a church. Some terraced hillsides
in the distance turned
labyrinthine green, an intricate backdrop

for songbirds that appeared
and disappeared
as awkwardly as a child's paper cutouts

threading in and out of trees.
We touch each other briefly
and depart. As if memory wasn't a wound to bear.

As if we could eat the fruit
and forget the garden.
Rugosas redolent in the summer night.

Years later, walking back
from dinner along
the bastion in Alghero. Swordfish

drizzled with virgin oil, rubbed with
mint and saffron.
Wild boar steamed in myrtle leaves.

Someone having a birthday,
"Tanti auguri a te,"
　　　the words rising in the piazza—

　　　And suddenly the light,
that light. *The sanctuary with*
　　　its silver offering bowls, the lepers singing.

　　　Here are the goblets filled with wine.
The smell of sunlight
　　　fading from the stones. Quietness that's solitude

　　　but not isolation. And the windows lit
with displays of red corals
　　　from just off the coast

　　　said to be the blood that streamed
from Medusa's severed neck
　　　when Perseus laid her head beside the sea.

DJENNÉ, MALI

Room full of barefoot tailors, open air
courtyard, the antique
sewing machines nattering on. Heat paired
with need, the slack
mouths gathering pollen, coughing while lime dust
drifts in the streets.
It's market day.
Shops fill and empty like lungs—
Ribbons of black flies against the rust.

Under the mud mosque, stands of printed cloth.
A woman selling hills of green powder
(alcove of shade)
takes my hand. Her palm blooms with feminine
leaves, a palimpsest of henna and skin.
Radiant palm to my palm—
Hot flowers with such patient faces.

ALMOST A FIGURE

Every time I see you I'm reminded of Akhmatova
describing Leningrad burning. The flames a funeral pyre

of feverish poppies; their reds a requiem for bone. I imagine
the disbelief, exquisite

fascination of fire and the Winter Palace consumed.

          People stuffing jewels in coat pockets and mouths
          everyone suddenly aware of what it means to be a
          body.

I wonder how many of them
          descending through the city

turned back to their houses. Locked themselves in

          and watched plumes of smoke sliding up
          to the sky
              weightless
                  ambivalent

          without grief, or need to hold any*thing* or

          any*one* at all.

     I was in Belfast, you were hospitalized and
tested. I kept dreaming of doctors with enormous hands
abusing flowers.
          And of a sericulture room, dimly lit

where the single
long filaments of silkworms
were drawn from empty cocoons
by machines—

My entomology professor once said:
On the cephalothorax of the brown recluse
there is a pattern like a violin.

Forgive me this old habit. There is a danger
in making suffering beautiful.

This is what I realized that night in that divided city.
After playing the wretched hostel piano, I wrote:

Dear N,

I want to cut off my hair
and tie it into brushes
so I can paint the city of Belfast
in its true humanity.

All day long I passed an artist's studio
where the clay arms and hands of women
were displayed in the window.

Small hands to hold such a city.

Love,
  K

GRANDFATHER OUTSIDE

There are sadnesses which cast in one's soul the shadows of monasteries.
                    —E. M. Cioran

We arrived too late for the sundial.
          The monks were bats circling
stone paths: we watched

the glow of their lamps in the garden
          as they pulled the onions
for our meal. That night I dreamt

you and I were walking
          underwater. Orange jellyfish
rose like suns. We couldn't speak.

So slowly, we moved together
          against the tide. Until you
disappeared into a submarine wood

not unlike the one bordering
          the monastery
that long night in Romania.

                    *

Near midnight, the monks sang
          through blue corridors of incense
as if tuning the dark

to the low note of their devotion.
          The halos of each painted saint
glowed like winter wheat.

They said they kept their mass
          through the dead of night
so that Christ, crying falcon,

plummeting alone
          through Gethsemane
would be caught by the threads

of a net so loyal it stretched
          backwards through time. I never knew
that days were held together by singing.

Or that those who suffered
          could be attended to
long after they had gone.

          *

Now, one year after your death
          the radio crackles Rachmaninoff—
a nocturne that won't end.

Alone in the sacristy, I found the ankle
          bone of John the Baptist. Displayed
in a carved foot of wood. I could

imagine his ghost walking those
          grounds. Wild in the garden, baptizing
piles of raw beets as they split in the sun.

Maybe tonight he'll bless me.
      With a simple gift, one a ghost could
give. Something like snow falling

over the morning you died. Emptying
      yourself into the exhausted
arms of a hospital bed.

OF THE BEACHCOMBERS UNDER AIRPLANE'S X

We wander up among sea oats with birds of paradise eyes. The sun
washes up like a dead goldfish.

*

A long row of empty beach houses staggers into the surf on salt-eaten legs,
wood weathered like the faces of long-dead kings.

We are wet with the night's freezing rain. We bury our shit like surgeons
in the cold sand of the dunes.

*

Then our eyes catch the tremor that could be some stray *obake*
shifting in the tattered grass. We stay and make a temple for him

of pink anemones. We drink the leftover wine. And we stand,
still at odds with the world, like distinguished topiaries.

THE ORANGES IN UGANDA

Walking together, Death and I
are shopping for *emicungwa*
at night, in the market.
Each careful pyramid of fruit
is stacked on cardboard, illuminated
by candles. Death's feet are bare
and covered with dirt
from the road.

We talk of small things.
How the mosque and the half moon
stand sentinel
against the bloody sky. That mangoes
will be in season soon.
I tell him I know why
people make love when they
come home from a funeral. Why the pull
of the body echoes the tides,
eyes wide as graves. The way the stamens
of a passion flower spin up,
defy their stem.

Thinking all the while,
fumbling with the prickly shapes of jackfruit
and their sticky sap. *Yesu,*
the death pulse ringing louder
than talking drums, viral in the blood.

Cloaked in barkcloth, Death
raises his ancestral spear, singing mouth full

of ulcers and steel. He has known the Tombs
of Kasubi,
Home of Kings.

The street children are out
stealing watches again.
There are no stars to behold.
Nkooye, Death says. *I am tired.*
He rises like a swallow
from the depth of grasses,
leaving a rip no word can cover.

RISK

In the dream, I am given a monkey heart
and told to be careful how I love
because of the resulting infection.
Suddenly a hard-boiled egg with no yolk,
I pitch down a great hill in a holy city,
past the flaming beakers of ethanol,
the lapis bowls in which Science
would peel me apart. And when I skid
into a fleshy patch of grass,
I unroll into a grub. A grub with the mind
of a girl, a girl with the lips of an insect.
A voice says, *Metamorphosis*
will make you ugly. I answer:
Radiance will change its name.
In the heat I squirm and shrug
out of my summer suit and breathless
split into a cotton dress. It is almost
evening. There are fireflies.
On the lawn of my childhood house,
an operating table, doctors,
a patient under a sheet. I walk up.
Under the webbing of IVs,
a surgeon hands me a silver comb
and I start brushing the patient's hair
like I did my mother's when I was a girl.
The nurse lifts the sheet.
It isn't my mother. It's the monkey.
I bend my ear to its dying lips
and it says: *You haven't much time—*
risk it all.

WATER CLOCKS

The singing of the blind school
        children and the
Mediterranean's flat expanse are metaphors

for every kind of solitude made
        forgivable by time.
The hillside museum with rows of empty

earthen vessels is full of it. A stillness
        so replete
it resembles something like intimacy.

A fullness only partially fathomed.
        Like water clocks
and sundials that allowed time to be

translated into elements: *droplets, shadows.*
        And the laughter
of bathers from the spiaggetta.

                        *

The train stops just outside of Naples
        where I buy a glass
of cold juice squeezed from tangerines

and walk into Pompeii. I couldn't have
        imagined the
magnitude of it. Brilliant pillars flush

with sky. Temples where sunlight
    streams white
and seems to radiate from inside

the stones. Certain histories require
    forgetfulness.
Others, strict belief. But I think

some histories live *us.* In the higher cities
    of the brain,
even the speechless ones are burning.

THREE

GHOST NETS

I

Yellow snapper, bright as egg yolk. I look at the sea and eat my toast.

Yesterday's lesson—the *jabonero de Cortés* or Cortez soapfish
when agitated
secretes a mucus that lathers like soap—

The fish, the scientists say, are gliding quietly into extinction. They hovered
last night at the edge of my half-dream, softening their fins to a point of pure

blur, pure erasure. "They lack a neck," says Aristotle, "their tail is continuous
with their body, except
in rays (raies) where it is long and slender; they do not have hands, or feet . . ."

II

The divers test the air as if still underwater. All day hunting
clams and scallops, snails and octopus.

      I've made pink lemonade with a bag of ice
from the gas station down the road.

In the kitchen, one diver begins to tell a story
      of his youth: sea turtles surging to shore

by the hundreds, gouging sand with muscled flippers to lay their eggs.

They arrived by night. And at the end of the nesting season,
they'd capture a turtle as she circled back to the sea. Cleave

her throat, hold a cup to catch the blood and drink
before cracking the plastron and removing the meat.

      Not what he says, but how he says it.
He speaks as if this was an act of love.

Green grubs dropping from palm fronds to the porch, the sour-sweet
of cheap lemonade.

      And always the dialectic of inside/outside—

III

Ask the blind how carefully we build our world on light.

Ask the octopus how the evolution of our eyes converged.

IV

I don't pretend to imagine the lives of women tending oyster crates
in estuaries at the edge of Sonora.

It's enough to follow the hand-painted sign of a mermaid
                                        peeling and peeling in the sand.

At the end of the road, the dunes roil with a pack of feral dogs
feasting on the carcass of a washed-up fin whale.

The tide seeps in with its pewter description,
                        simple and flat under halophytic grasses. We sit

under *palapas* that rustle their shaggy hair,
                                as if clearing the air of meaning.

All living is brushwork, you say.

Watching the women wade to the crates with their Styrofoam floats,
the oysters quivering in their cups of flesh and lime.

V

"Not perfection," the sea hisses, "but originality." The innards of a blue-eyed scallop scraped onto a plastic Safeway bag. Soul and meat—

VI

We were remembering the first
        time we swam with parrotfish. Drinking wine
the color of rose granite. Some varietal from

Greece. Your grey cat was stalking
        grasshoppers beneath the pomegranate tree.
What wakes us *hears* us, I said.

And we looked at the clouds
        which were shredding themselves
as awkwardly as children learning left-handed scissors.

VII

"Camarones," the fishermen cry,
from the pier where shrimp and spiny oysters shine

on broken slabs of ice,
                              children flying cellophane
kites until the wind stops, until the clouds drain away

                    into a blue as pale as paper.
Yesterday was boojum trees and the glassy lavas
of the Pinacates.

            Today the photograph of the Seri woman in sepia,
bare-breasted in a skirt of sewn-together pelican wings.

Dust settles on the street, on the man sharpening his machete
at the *Cocos Helados* stand.

                  Every day, it happens like this.
We emerge from the pale nets of sleep like ghost shrimp
in the estuaries—
            The brain humming its electric language.

Touching something in a state of becoming.

VIII

I remember Agassiz and the sunfish. The dream in which each
breath is a perfect sphere, in which the only explanation is
                                        pink and voltaic—

life! Sealed inside itself like barnacles at high tide.

Pay attention. To the edges, the carved pumice heads
        seem to say, from the ledge near the stove.

Scrubbing cactus pads, cutting them in strips to fry with eggs.

Down the road, large piles of murex shells—
                        their insides like the insides of ears.

All that quiet. Like dreaming you're standing on water
        but not hearing the water.

The sunfish, decomposed. Shoreline crumbling like bleached sugar.
Re-making sand as candy skulls
                        for *El Día de los Muertos.*

IX

Katherine—

heliaster! All night, the seals barking. We wake to sun stars
stretching in the tide pools
                              and the stench
of the rotting sea lion carcass with the plastic Coke bottle
lodged inside its throat.

The day you sawed off the head of the dead dolphin
with your mother,
              you were trying to get past the abstraction of death

to the singularity of dying. You believed the skull
was scaffolding meant for study

before the body broke down into its customary ash,
                              echoes looping in empty arches—

Because there are times when you swim at night, your arms leave

trails in the water. So many dinoflagellates switching on,
for a moment the darkness after your body is a trail of green light.

Then it vanishes.

X

The blankets were wet, but we dragged them anyway
to the dunes where we drank bitter coffee

and peeled cold, boiled eggs. In the distance, bonfires.
The stars opening and shutting like tiny fly-traps

with their green ashed-out, inked-over. The stillness enough
to hear pistol shrimp snap in the tide pools.

Each time the intimacy becomes greater, the vocabulary less.

XI

Then the one-armed baker at the *panadería,* spruced in his lemon-
yellow *guayabera,* such constant motif of startled

        gold, and gritty streets with tourist-shop

curtains of freeze-dried seahorses, starfish stale and goose-fleshed
as pages of Braille.

Memory. The invention
        of meaning. Our minds with deeps
        where only symbols creep.

The gulls cartwheeling, screaming as they shred the washed-up diapers.
At the shoreline, froth of *Callinectes* crabs. Greek for beautiful swimmer.

FOUR

LANDSCAPE TILTING TOWARDS OBLIVION

Ah, this—my much loved country
of trilobites and trembling lotus,
of black pools full of snapping turtles
and newspaper boats
made by children never wrongly kissed.

Nothingness feeds me supper: a lacerated
tulip, a rhubarb shard that gleams.

Why do some plants wear human faces?
What makes stars shiver in their
burning coats?
   Love, the rain here
stains sundials all night. *Docet umbra,*
one is inscribed. *Incipit* another's signed.

BROKE THE LUNATIC HORSE

The Milky Way sways its back
across all of wind-eaten America
like a dusty saddle tossed
over your sable, lunatic horse.
All the plains are dark.
All the stars are cowards:
they lie to us about their time of death
and do nothing but dangle
like a huge chandelier
over nights when our mangled sobs
make the dead reach for their guns.
I must be one of the only girls
who still dreams in green gingham, sees snow
as *a steel pail's falling of frozen nails*
like you said through pipe smoke
on the cabin porch one night. Dear one,
there are no nails more cold
than those that fix you
underground. I thought I saw you
in the moon of the auditorium
after my high school dance.
Without you, it's still hard to dance.
It's even hard to dream.

PIANO LESSONS

Most nights I watch the kids
        in the alley eat large plates of rice
                and fish. I love their industrious

mother who sweeps
        these sitting steps twice a day.
                Not quite as often

her letters are returned
        unopened and stamped with red ink.
                Those times, I can't

explain her eyes.
        It makes me think of the keys
                on this piano that refuse to sound.

I imagine these are
        my lover's apologies and
                find delight in a chord

made of only one note.
        The weight of the silence
                is clearest when you play

Bach, p. 134, Prelude 22:
        This very ornate prelude is often
                in five voices, and

of great pathos.
        The man upstairs just lost
                his wife to cancer.

He is moving himself out
         of the apartment by
                  throwing something new

from the window every
         day. Sometimes there are
                  enormous crashes on the balcony.

Last week he dragged
         his bathtub outside.
                  I found him curled in it,

rocking, as if on a toy horse.
         I miss him singing to
                  his cat in French.

Now other little ceremonies
         mark time's passing:
                  the baby starling fallen

from its nest last week,
         Clarissa's postcard from China:
                  Dear S, Matthew

and I have fallen in love
         with the country and think
                  we're going to stay.

Guilin is lovely. A man
         stopped me on the bridge
                  last week to give me

a small Buddha carved from a pine stick
         even in the pouring rain.
                  Last night the baby

kicked so hard I
        doubled over in
                a thistle patch and started

tearing plants out
        by the roots. Clarissa,
                I'm scared to have this baby.

The man upstairs told me
        about a hang glider
                who survived a fall from hundreds

of feet into a field
        of poisonous snakes. He died of snakebite.
                I think it was his son.

SOLARIUM

The pomegranates are blurs of rouge
in the sky's tarnished mirror.

The city, bleary with heat. Each day the eyes
of my cat assemble a more precocious gold.

We press our blackened flesh against a sky so bright. I hold
her in my arms at the fading windows.

We gaze together at nothing in particular,
down an avenue that leans so far her tawny eyes

gutter out. In my laboratory, immortal cancer cells
divide and divide. The pomegranates

are almost ripe. Some splintered open the way
all things fragment—into something fundamental.

Either everything's sublime or nothing is.

METAMORPHOSIS

It is astounding how little the ordinary person notices butterflies.
                                              —Nabokov

We dredge the stream with soup strainers
and separate dragonfly and damselfly nymphs—
their eyes like inky bulbs, jaws snapping
at the light as if the world was full of
tiny traps, each hairpin mechanism
tripped for transformation. Such a ricochet
of appetites insisting *life, life, life* against
the watery dark, the tuberous reeds. Tell me—
how do they survive passage? I rinse our cutlery
in the stream. Heat so heavy it hurts the skin.
The drone of wild bees. We swim through cities
buried in seawater, we watch the gods decay.
We dredge the gods of other civilizations.
The sun, for example. Before the deity became a
star. *Jasper scarabs excavated from the hearts of*
kings. Daylight's blue-green water pooling at the
foot of falls. Sandstones where the canyon spills
its verdant greens in vines. Each lunar
resurrection, each helix churning in the cells
of a sturgeon destined for spawning—
Not equilibrium, but buoyancy. A hallway
with a thousand human brains carved out of crystal.
Quiet prisms until the sunlight hits.

PATIENCE

Once a month
when the moon loses everything
Don Max takes a chair
to the edge of the sea.
Black sand beach and green-backed heron.
The moon
casts off her milk glass earrings.
I am nothing, she says, but black and white.
I keep losing my face.
Don Max feels for his pipe in his pocket.
Takes it, knocks it against his palm.
I am old! She cries. I get gooseflesh
in the dark. Don Max is looking for his tobacco.
Don Max has found a match.
You don't know how hard it is
to come back from nothing.
Don Max smiles and lights up.
I keep making the same mistakes, she says.
I think you should leave me, she says.
Through smoke, she watches Don Max
fold a strip of seaweed into a grasshopper.
Leave me for your own good! She demands.
Don Max has set the grasshopper in the sand.
Besides, I am too beautiful.
She speaks it as though it makes her sad.
I'll find other lovers. I will
forget you.

MASCULINE/FEMININE

The material suggests ... that many, if not all, of the personality traits which we have called
masculine or feminine are as lightly linked to sex as are the clothing, the manners, and the form
of head-dress that a society at a given period assigns to either sex.
—Margaret Mead

In a dream, Baudelaire comes to me as a blue-faced baboon.
He is skinny and wearing a look of such intensity it could make stars

sprout antennae. I tell him about M. Mead, but he interrupts me.
Yes, he says impatiently. Forget the flawed anthropologist.

Can't the cat be both animal and mistress with its pelt of electric fur?
I say that my mother wakes each morning a red-tailed hawk.

My father, a purple urchin on a silver dish. We hear the cactus whisper
pollinate me furry moth. The rattlesnake at our feet reminds us that he sees

the world in infrared. And then the clouds, which in my language
are neither male nor female, come to pin up my hair with their tiny torn tufts.

IN A CEMETERY BY THE SEA:
ONE DEFINITION OF A CIRCLE

You lie on the stone slab of St. Caomhan's grave,

the rain inking around us. On your forehead

                                   you place the purple blade of the scallop.

                            It shines like a watermark between your eyes.

This pilgrim's badge, the islanders told us,

                                was supposed to heal you.

        Instead, it makes your body transparent.

Runes carved in the stone beneath you I read

as one of the early histories of our refractory bodies;

            I understand St. Caomhan was a fisherman who longed as I do

                              for the arms of a God.

Early that morning, I watched the postman on his bicycle delivering letters.
Two wheels turning so slowly over the cobbles,

                              I thought he had to fall.

Things that are equal to the same things are equal to each other, says Euclid.
Here, the morning birds are equal to the dawn.

The stone wall to the shore, where jellyfish like terrible offerings
present themselves each day to rot,

sheer centers surrounded by violet circles.
I trace them as *he* would have—beginning to end.

NOTES

The translation for G. A. Bécquer's "Rima XXII" is provided courtesy of Carlos Gallego. Its use as an epigraph is inspired by B. Brant Bynum's *The Romantic Imagination in the Works of Gustavo Adolfo Bécquer* (Chapel Hill: University of North Carolina Press, 1994).

"A Lime Tree for San Cristóbal": The italicized section is excerpted from Charles Darwin's *Galapagos Notebook* (Darwin Collection at Down House).

"Study for Love's Body": Part II takes as its source Douglas Cooper's *Paul Gauguin: 45 Lettres à Vincent, Théo et Jo van Gogh* (Lausanne: La Bibliothèque des Arts, 1983).

"Landscape with Yellow Birds," "Architecture in Ruins," "Almost a Figure," and "The Gardens in Tunisia" are titles borrowed—and sometimes slightly altered—from the visual art of Paul Klee.

"Crypsis and Mimicry": Certain details were informed by Lyle Saxon et al., *Gumbo Ya-Ya: Folk Tales of Louisiana* (Gretna Louisiana: Pelican Publishing Co., 1987).

"Djenné, Mali" is for Donna Swaim and Michael Bonine.

"Lake of Little Birds" and "Risk" are for Alex.

"Ghost Nets": Lost or discarded gill nets, sometimes called "ghost nets" for the way they continue to indiscriminately trap and kill organisms from seabirds to porpoises, are one of several fishing by-products that have been devastating to marine ecosystems worldwide.

The quote from Aristotle in "Ghost Nets (I)" comes from George Cuvier and Theodore W. Pietsch's *Historical Portrait of the Progress of Ichthyology, from Its Origins to Our Time* (Baltimore: Johns Hopkins University Press, 1995). The reference to Agassiz and the sunfish in "Ghost Nets (VIII)" was informed by Ezra Pound's *ABC of Reading* (New York: New Directions Publishing Co., 1960).

"Ghost Nets (I)" is for DAT (Donald A. Thomson); "Ghost Nets (II)" is for Rick Boyer and Peggy Turk Boyer; "Ghost Nets (IV)" is for Chris Impey; "Ghost Nets (V)" is for Morgan Lucas Schuldt; "Ghost Nets (VI)" is for Ann Jones; "Ghost Nets (VIII)" is for Lois Epperson-Gale; "Ghost Nets (IX)" is for Heather Green; "Ghost Nets (X)" is for Alyssa and Dennis Rosemartin, and "Ghost Nets (XI)" is for Tom Wilkening.

"Patience" is for Max Rojas.